HARK!
A
VAGRANT

Published by Jonathan Cape 2011

2 4 6 8 10 9 7 5 3 1

Comics – excluding a few originals – originally published at www.harkavagrant.com

First published in Great Britain in 2011 by
Jonathan Cape
Random House, 20 Vauxhall Bridge Road,
London SW1V 2SA

www.vintage-books.co.uk

Addresses for companies within The Random House Group Limited can be found at:
www.randomhouse.co.uk/offices.htm

The Random House Group Limited Reg. No. 954009

A CIP catalogue record for this book is available from the British Library

ISBN 9780224094146

The Random House Group Limited supports The Forest Stewardship Council (FSC®), the leading international forest certification organisation. Our books carrying the FSC label are printed on FSC® certified paper. FSC is the only forest certification scheme endorsed by the leading environmental organisations, including Greenpeace. Our paper procurement policy can be found at www.randomhouse.co.uk/environment http://www.randomhouse.co.uk/environment

MIX
Paper from
responsible sources
FSC
www.fsc.org
FSC® C016897

Printed and bound in Great Britain by MPG Books Ltd, Bodmin, Cornwall

HARK! A VAGRANT

KATE BEATON

JONATHAN CAPE • LONDON

Let me take a minute to dedicate this book to my parents, because it's the right thing to do with your first book, and no one deserves it better. Some time ago I packed my history degree into a suitcase and said goodbye to the world of working in museums for low pay and limited opportunity, and said hello to the world of being a cartoonist, which, as we all know, is lucrative and glamorous. I had been drawing comics since university, when I would put off essays for history classes to draw comics for the student paper. Not that I didn't enjoy my classes, rather the opposite, but you and I both know that there are always better things to be doing than writing an essay that's due by the end of the week. It turned out, to my great luck, that what I really had a knack for was putting the two together—history and comics. That's what started all this, in any case. I think comics about topics like history or literature can be amazing educational tools, even at their silliest. So if you learn or look up a thing or two after reading these comics, and you've enjoyed them, then I will be more than pleased! If you're just in it for the silly stuff, then there is plenty of that to go around, too. While I have the chance, I want to thank a few people. First, the authors whose work I read—whether it was a novel to be parodied, historical research, a comic book, or any number of things. I am forever in debt to those who have inspired, educated, and entertained me, and given life to my comics. Secondly, thanks to everyone who has supported me in this from the beginning—you friends, you family, you readers. You know, the thing that keeps you doing a job like this is the idea that there is someone out there who is actually going to like what you're making, and I can't believe I'm fortunate enough to have fantastic people who enjoy the loony pictures I like to draw. I'll keep it up for as long as I can, or until the museum world calls and begs to have me back…and they have a dental plan.

GET ME OFF THIS FREAKING MOOR

Anne, why are you writing books about how alcoholic losers ruin people's lives? Don't you see that romanticizing douchey behavior is the proper literary convention in this family! *Honestly*. Losers who ruin people's lives are who we want to dream about at night.

A HISTORY DEBATE

A MAGICAL DAY

My father is an excellent gardener and can grow enough vegetables to keep us fed all through the winter. Turnips are amazing because they are root vegetables, so if you pick them and put them in soil in the cellar, they last for ages and ages. For more information about turnips, see every day of my childhood.

If Susan B. Anthony were on *Sex and the City*, do you think she would be a Carrie, a Miranda, a Charlotte, or a Samantha? Definitely a Samantha.

JUST DON'T FLY DURING RED APRIL

In WWI, pilots were the cool new thing. So exciting! Flying aces! Nothing like that had ever existed before. That's why people like Billy Bishop could become a star and inspire all the young bros to sign up. The only real drawback was that for 99 percent of new recruits, an engine would blow up in their faces two minutes after taking off for the first time. Beyond that, it's a great life. Just don't fly during Red April, boys.

TEAM BOLIVAR

Sucre was Bolívar's right hand man for sure (matching hairdos and everything), but I think he had a much different approach to leadership. I really wonder how different the outcome of the Spanish American Wars of Independence would have been if Sucre hadn't been assassinated just as he was poised to become Bolívar's obvious successor. I wish I had something funny to say now.

PEARY I THOUGHT WE WERE FRIENDS

Peary got himself some frostbitten feet and someone else drove that sled and *that* is *that*. Now, these two weren't Canadian, but it is always interesting to note that at the very same time that Canadian immigration was insisting that black people couldn't handle the cold, a black man was the first non-native person to set foot on the North Pole. Don't you love it when the irony is that good? Matthew Henson gets his due these days; it only took a century or something. A nod to Ootah, Egingwah, Seegloo, and Ooqueah as well.

WATSON I MISS YOU

Poor Doctor Watson gets a bad hand in a lot of on-screen portrayals and parodies, and more than a few people have a mental image of him as a fat old dodderer. Unfair! We all look kind of stupid next to Sherlock Holmes, but come on.

ANOTHER CASE OF WATSONS

Here's the thing about a homosexual relationship between Holmes and Watson: you are never going to prove it. It just isn't in the books, explicitly. It would be rad if it were, but it's not, so now we are going to have arguments with no end because, maybe maybe maybe maybe. Eventually the idea that these two were hookin' up between the pages gets so popular that people who never read the books will argue, "Yeah man, of course they were!" That's popular culture for you! It's interesting. Between you and me, I much prefer Gay Watson to Stupid Watson (I mean, obviously). What Watson does in his spare time is his business. Now solve me some damn crimes, boys!

I'll make one of those YA series where adults believe what teens tell them. Except instead of fake teens, mine will have real ones because real teens don't give a shit about anything.

Nothing says "Hallowe'en" like teens being punks and throwing shit. They're on the job here, but who knows what for. They're not doing it anyway, whatever it is.

Not their employer's office, another one! Oh you little teenage ne'er-do-wells. Like most teens, they go to school, but much like the ones who enroll in art class because it's easy, sometimes they are also not there.

DO SOMETHING ABOUT IT

The Pony is an enduring symbol of…something in whatever country he lives in. It would be fascinating to know what that is or what the people see in him. Clearly though, I am not going to tell you.

PONY

The pony returns! It does a job for the King, I think. But that could all be in the King's head.

ANNE of SLEEVES

In *Anne of Green Gables*, the plucky young orphan grows from a child with a wild imagination and a tongue she cannot hold into a sophisticated and responsible young lady. If there were no scene where she gets the puff-sleeved dress she pines for, I think there would have been a chapter where she slaughters the whole town.

Finally, after years of hard work, Handel broke through with his first major hit, "Safety Dance," and he totally ruled the eighties!!

THE SCOTTISH PLAY

They say the real Macbeth was a pretty decent fellow and a good ruler, and he'd probably have a bone to pick with Shakespeare over character assassination. He'd have to get in line behind Richard III though, whom I have heard (from certain Elizabethan sources) was an ugly hunchbacked troll.

UNSEX ME, SEX ME

THE GAG COMES BACK

HELL IS MURKY

MACBETH WANTS TO HEAR IT AGAIN

LAY ON MACDUFF, WITH MOTIFS

GOOD QUESTION

THE RETURN of ANNABEL LEE

When I read *Annabel Lee* and listen to that narrator pine and whine and pine, I think "Man, Annabel? You put up with this loser?" It's okay to pine now and then, but the man needs a hobby that isn't lying beside her grave and moaning. Then I wonder, "What if Annabel came back and she was just as lame as he was?" It's like they say: be careful what you wish for.

COME DREAM WITH ME

It's true that Jules Verne wrote what we may call "fan mail" to Edgar Allan Poe. By fan mail, of course, I mean a full-on sequel to one of Poe's books. Perhaps Poe doesn't get enough credit for influencing science fiction, since many people think about ravens, madness, and other dreary things when the name "Poe" comes up. Don't get me wrong, the man could write a dirge of a paragraph, a hell of a wah-wah cryfest. But he could also write about hot air balloons.

RETURN OF VERNE

Jules Verne made a famous rant about H.G. Wells once that basically threw a fit over Wells making up whatever he liked about spaceships and other devices. Wells wrote about these things without explicitly describing how they functioned, and he didn't power them with steam or coal or anything that made sense in 1899. Jules didn't like that! "It's science fiction," he said, "so where's the science?!" In response, Wells possibly called Verne "an old fusspot."

ONE OF YOU WILL DO IT BY GOD

Dynasties the monarchy way are so easy! You have a kid? Great, they are next in line for the best throne in the Throne Room. In America it's hard because you have to "prove yourself" and maybe people have to "vote for you" and that's difficult! No one knew that better than Joe Kennedy Sr., who trained his wife to give birth to the United States Senate.

PROTÉGÉ

Beethoven had an Immortal Beloved but no children to pass his wisdom onto. I guess he figured his nephew would have to do. Unfortunately for everyone in this comic, talent is not a thing you can pass on, nor passion for any one thing. Writing a fantastic symphony is not like baking Mom's secret pie recipe, even if Mom's secret pie recipe is pretty darn good.

CRIMINAL MASTERMINDS

I have no idea why I made them talk so funny, but that is what happens sometimes in this crazy comics world. I guess it is because it's a comic about two weirdos! Here we meet Burke and Hare toward the end of their killing spree, a period that may be described as "unbelievably sloppy" and also "lazy." Still, they had an impact on medical history (medical cadavers for everyone!), and perhaps not every harebrained criminal may lay claim to this.

Some fast comics. Out they come, pen to paper, lickety split.

CELEBRATE THE BEST WAY

Canadians are their most Canadian on three occasions: when they've left the country, when Olympic Hockey is going on, and on Canada Day. The rest of the time it's a toss-up on whether they're feeling patriotic or if they just feel like tossing the whole enterprise and moving to Miami. Anyway, what is a celebration of national unity in this country without a little national disunity? It's only proper, traditionally.

BE A HERO

Wonder Woman has spent a lifetime as one of the biggest deals in comics, and yet I think it's universally agreed that no one has been able to truly "get" her character right. If that were me, I'd probably be pissed.

WORLD'S FINEST

IT'S IN HIS NATURE

WONDER WOMAN RETURNS

Weren't most superheroes first created to fight Nazis? Guess they had to find something else to do after the war.

ONCE UPON A

Remember when you found out that fairy tales were much deeper and darker than the Disney cartoons you knew made them out to be? I mean, Cinderella's stepsisters are punished *how* in Grimm's version? You were like, "Damn!" when you read that. Perhaps you thought, "Maybe that's not such a bad thing, to jazz it up a bit?" Perhaps you even thought that the elves in *The Elves and the Shoemaker* were a major bore and would be better if they were members of the band Kiss.

BRUNEL IS TIRED OF THESE TIME TRAVELING ASSHOLES

ISAMBARD KINGDOM BRUNEL! WOW! CHECK MY AWESOME STEAMPUNK GOGGLES

WHAT DO THEY DO

CHECK IT

gears

TELL ME THEY DO SOMETHING

I PUT A SHITLOAD OF COGS AND WATCHES ON MY BOOT

FIRING SQUAD

DO YOU HAVE ANY LAST WORDS

yes

I DID IT FOR LOVE!

OH!

FOR... ME?

POW POW POW POW

SICK MANUSCRIPT BRO

ALSO IT IS MY PERSONAL FETISH

WWII HIPSTER BATALLION

WWII HIPSTER BATTALION

HIPSTERS RUIN EVERYTHING, PT. 1

It's funny when people complain about how hipsters ruined this or that as though if hipsters would just go away, the problem would be solved and you could go back to wearing plaid shirts like you did before they were ruined for everyone. Directionless youths have always appropriated things and made them annoying! You have it easy, oh reader! The Beats had walking caricatures to deal with, and Goethe had suicidal poet dandies on his doorstep.

HIPSTERS RUIN EVERYTHING, PT. 2

The Incroyables and Merveilleuses were ironic hipsters years before their time. What they wore was once a political statement, but then they gave up on making statements, and that was a statement.

TUDORAMA

It's weird when television and movies think that in order to reach a modern audience, they need to sex up history. Sexy people did live in the past, and they had sex! Maybe that's not enough. Someone needs to build a time machine and go tell William Cecil that he may have been a crack statesman, but if he wants us to give a shit about him, he better start hitting the gym.

THE DEATH OF GENERAL BROCK

At Queenston Heights there is a stunning monument to a man who would not order his men anywhere he would not lead them. Somehow, mysteriously, this man got himself shot by a sniper. By mysteriously, of course, I mean that everyone was largely dressed the same, except for the fellow in front with the giant hat, big brass buttons, and, oh I don't know, rippling epaulettes. And anyway, of course you're going to shoot that guy.

STRANGER

SAL I DON'T LIKE THE LOOK OF THAT FELLA WHO JUST CAME IN

ME NEITHER

IF SOMEONE AROUND HERE DON'T TELL ME WHERE THE BATHROOM IS MY ASS IS GOING TO EXPLODE

OH

I CAME FOR THE DICK JOKES

DID YOU CATCH THE LATEST SHAKESPEARE?

DAMNED GOOD, IT WAS DAMNED GOOD

EXCELLENT USE OF METAPHOR AND... PATHETIC FALLACY?

GREAT LITERATURE TO BE SURE

BUT WHAT I QUITE LIKED WERE THE PUNS

I **REALLY** ENJOYED THE PUNS

IT'S HOW WE DID IT BACK THEN

BUT I WASN'T THE **ONLY** ONE AFTER YOUR GRANDMOTHER IN THOSE DAYS

I REMEMBER ONE YOUNG FELLOW, OH HE WAS VERY PERSISTENT

SO! I KILLED HIM MYSELF

GRANDPA!

SUBSTITUTE TEACHER

I WANT TO PUT A STOP TO THIS FAKE NAME BUSINESS RIGHT NOW!

"TITS PALMER"? DO YOU GUYS THINK I'M AN IDIOT?

YOU'VE UPSET TITS!

DON'T CRY TITS

WRONG ISLAND

BIG BUSINESS

BEST FRIENDS FOREVER

OH MY **GOD** YOU GUYS, I'M CARRIE, YOU'RE SAMANTHA, YOU'RE CHARLOTTE AND YOU'RE MIRANDA!

OH MY GOD IT'S SO TRUE!

I KNOW!

UM

YOU HAVE TO **LEAVE**

MESSIN' WITH YOUR KIDS

GO TO YOUR ROOM FOR AN HOUR!

NO!

YOU HEARD ME!

FINE.

NO!

THEN YOUR FATHER AND I ARE GOING TO WALK AROUND THE HOUSE NAKED FOR AN HOUR.

THAT'S RIGHT

NEWS FROM THE FRONT

A BAD AFFAIR

REGRETS

I MARRIED A
MANCHILD:
2063

DO YOU REMEMBER THE LOOK ON OUR SON'S FACE THE DAY HE GOT MARRIED

NOT REALLY

DO YOU REMEMBER THUNDERCATS

THAT WAS SUCH A GOOD SHOW

STUPID ROOSTER COMICS

LADAYS

AWE YEAH GIRL

YOU WANT DIS

51

THE OLD FOX

Is Montcalm less memorable because he lost the Battle of the Plains of Abraham to Wolfe? Unfair—I like Montcalm. All you need to know to like him as well is that his last letter to his wife reads, "I think I should have given up all my honors to be back with you, but the king must be obeyed; the moment when I shall see you again will be the finest of my life. Good-bye my heart, I believe I love you more than ever." What I am saying is that I want a romance novel with Montcalm on the cover and I want it now. He got one of those epic-death paintings eventually. It's okay.

EVERY LADY SCIENTIST WHO EVER DID ANYTHING TILL NOW

Rosalind! Don't let 'em get you down. The trouble with reading about any given woman who was born before your mom is that yes, sometimes, they were hilarious, powerful, tough, loud, etcetera, etcetera—all good comic making material! But then sometimes, man, the main thing about them is that they just got screwed, big time. Here's to all the old time ladies of science, and their ideas that were worth stealing.

AN EDUCATION

INTERVENTION

THE LATEST FASHIONS

CHARLES' POETRY

RADIUM EYES

THE TRUE FAITH

SCOUNDRELLY

Lord Lovat (Simon Fraser, born 1667—there are about a million Simon Fraser Lord Lovats) really epitomizes how reading Scottish history can make you want to tear your eyeballs out, or laugh because it's so nutty that it could pass as a farce. Either the people involved are disastrously loyal, or disastrously duplicitous. Everything is a disaster, but it's a hell of a ride. Lord Lovat was the last man to lose his head in Great Britain. I suppose, depending on whom you talk to, he deserved the honour.

Canadian stereotypes are either hilarious and amazing or stupid and embarrassing, depending on whom you ask. But I can't help myself. I love our silly stereotypes. Anyone who gets upset because too many people think their country is exceedingly polite needs to rethink their priorities. I want to apologize to anyone who is offended by that statement.

BIRTHDAY

SOH - RY

FINALLY THE RIGHT LEADER

ST. FRANCIS AND THE BIRDS

Catholic children are usually brought up with picture books of Saints; sometimes they have a favorite one. Many have super scary stories, like, "Saint So-and-So was ripped to pieces and consumed by hot flames." You know, stuff kids can relate to. Consequently, a lot of children like St. Francis of Assisi the best because his deal is that he is always pictured surrounded by a load of animals and no one chopped his head off.

THE BRAVE CREW OF THE NAUTILUS BATTLE THE MONSTROUS SQUID

The Nautilus was actually attacked by a "poulpe," which is an octopus, but the description sounds something like a squid, and it's usually translated as "squid." Does that make a difference? If a creature from the depths were attacking your ship, would you really care if it was an octopus or a squid, or would you just pull the hatch down over your head and try to remember how to pray? There are no atheists in foxholes, or in submarines beset by many-legged monsters.

PERIL

Thus did the Vikings terrorize the coast of Britain, among other places, joyously taking for themselves shiny trinkets and the newest styles in leggings, delighting in the suffering of others as they filled their pockets with scrunchies and fashion magazines.

MATRICIDE

There are some funny things in *The Life Of Nero*, if you like your maniac emperors that way. Pretty well all accounts of how Nero went about murdering his mother are hilariously awful in their own right—collapsible boat, anyone?—and the notion that he thought her ghost was after him is also good. On top of this, he had a neck beard, and according to Suetonius, he had a mullet and smelled bad.

15th CENTURY PEASANT ROMANCE COMICS

WELL NEITHER HAS SHE

TAKE ME AWAY

Back in the day, things were harder, you know? Love was harder. One day your sweetheart is here, the next they get one of those diseases we only read about in *Ripley's Believe It Or Not!*

FOR THE GLORY OF LOVE

OR MAYBE LIVE TILL YOU'RE 40

OR BEAR BAITING

SEVERAL INCONGRUITIES IN THIS ONE

CREDIT WHERE CREDIT IS DUE

These days Tesla is enjoying a belated surge in popularity. Everyone seems to be on Tesla's side now, against Edison; whereas before, Edison was the hero and Tesla was some nut job making a different lightbulb. Edison is getting to be well known as the jerk he totally was! But let us never forget: he wasn't the only one, as Marconi demonstrates for us. I bet there is a ton of shit Tesla invented that got stolen by other people. Probably cool things like skateboards and helicopters. Patent your inventions, kids.

GOREYS

Edward Gorey made many a nice book in his day, and on top of this, designed many a nice book cover. We're going to do a little exercise with some of them. You take a book, and then you guess what the story inside of it is based on the info you get from the cover. Because, you know, that's just how books work.

WHEN WILLIAM BUTLER YEATS WAS BORN HE WAS A GIANT BIRD!!

CRAAA

EVERYONE WAS LIKE **WHOAA** BUT THEN HE WROTE SOME POEMS

CRAAAH

THESE ARE PRETTY GOOD

THERE I CAME UPON AN ENCHANTED WOOD

AND THE MAGICAL SLUTS OF THE FOREST

HELLO

HI

OH WHAT AN ADVENTU WE

GRANDPA'S STORIES ARE **NOT TO BE LISTENED TO**

WELL YOU'VE WON.
YOU CAN HAVE SPAIN,
OR PARTY ISLAND

PARTY
ISLAND!

WHAT— THERE'S
NOTHING HERE!
PARTY ISLAND **SUCKS**

YEAH THEY NAMED
IT PARTY ISLAND
AS A JOKE.

IRONIC LIKE

WHAT HAVE
I DONE

IT WAS FUNNY BUT
I GUESS YOU HAD
TO BE THERE

PATTY CAKE
PATTY CAKE B-

TROILUS...

WE'RE TOO **OLD**
FOR THIS GAME

LET'S HAVE
SEX

NO! AGAIN!

BUT-

PATTY CAKE
PATTY CAKE
BAKER'S MAN!

LAURA

Laura Secord looms so largely as a Canadian Hero (or as a box of chocolates depending on what your interests are), but during her lifetime, she fought until she was an old lady for anyone to recognize what she did at all. That sort of thing happened all the time; they can make a book about it called *Bummer History*. Good chocolates though.

THE ONE COMMANDMENT

HELP ME HANDSOME DOCTOR

THE WISEST

OCEANS IN NEED

There's an idea out there that Aquaman is lame as far as superheroes go, but I'm not sure. I read a bit about Aquaman growing a beard and having a harpoon hand and living in a cave and talking to spirits or something, and thought, "How can anyone not like this guy? This crazy dude, living under the water?" Anyway, that is the only version of Aquaman that I know, but I am really into it.

PIRATES

YOU AND I COULD MAKE A BAD VENGEANCE

TATTOO COMPARISONS

Pirates are overdone these days. If you agree, please do not read the comics above.

I WANTED TO GET INTO FORENSICS BECAUSE OF CSI

NEMESIS MINE

AUSTEN MANIA

Jane Austen has transcended "fandom," I think. Now there is an Austen culture. It's never certain what we should make of it. What is it about Mister Darcy that drove readers wild? What is it about the manners and conversation in the stories that inspired a craze of popular parodies? Why not a culture around, I don't know, *Madame Bovary*? Jane, either you are blessed, or you are cursed.

Are any of us really surprised that there is so much Darcy/Elizabeth fan fiction out there? Fan fiction was created for this. Aching stares from across the room can only go so far, if you know what I'm sayin'.

THE ROCHESTER WEDDING PARTY

In the various essays out there titled "In Defense of Mr. Rochester," we are to understand that keeping a nutty wife in your attic was a reasonable alternative to the asylums of the day. Fair enough. However, after much consideration, we the jury still find Mr. Rochester to be a creepy wife-hiding weirdo. We know Jane is coming back to him eventually, but we really wish Bertha could make a break for it.

JANE EYRE

GOOD TO BE UGLY

THE SOLUTION

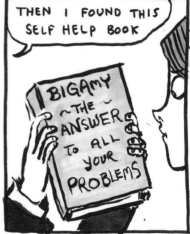

What the heck is happening out on those moors? Is it like when you're out in your boat for too long and you start to lose it, and you think you see a beautiful mermaid, but it's really a manatee? Then you've made out with it and you don't know why? We only want Jane to be happy though, because she had a pretty rough go in life and she's a smart cookie. We'll let her have Mr. Rochester because she loves him, even though he might be a manatee.

WHAT WERE YOU THINKING

TRUEST DECLARATION

JEALOUSY

HAPPY ENDING

DIRTY WORDS

TYCHO

VICTORIANS

Remember when you were small and you would lookup all the dirty words in the dictionary? If it were a good dictionary, it had at least three, and then you and your friends would laugh because dirty words are hi-larious. I resist the urge to put them in comics most of the time these days, but sometimes you just gotta (sorry Mom!).

WHAT A STUPID COMIC I HAVE MADE

FRANKLIN, AMERICA NEEDS
YOU TO INVENT MORE
AMAZING AND USEFUL THINGS

NO

I'M DEVOTING ALL MY
TIME TO WHORES FROM
NOW ON

WHAT COULD HAVE
BEEN

NEMESIS RETURNS

SIR WE'RE TAKING
MORE WATER THAN
WE CAN HANDLE

THAT LAST CANNON
VOLLEY WAS TOO
MUCH

WE'RE GOING **DOWN**
IT'S JUST **LIKE** HIM
TOO, YOU KNOW?

MYTHICAL TEENS

ICARUS MY SON, THESE WINGS ARE A PRIVILEGE, NOT A RIGHT. DO NOT FLY TOO CLOSE TO THE SUN.

YO ICARUS DO IT

HA HA MAN DO IT

HA HA YOU GUYS NOT IN FRONT OF MY DAD

PLEASE DO NOT LISTEN TO YOUR LOSER FRIENDS

PUG COMICS

WHO'S MOMMY'S BABY WITH A SQUISHY FACE! LITTLE CUTE SQUASHED IN FACE!

95

HOW DID YOU GET THIS NUMBER

How did he get that number?! A few liberties may have been taken in this comic. Bell and Watson probably did not have a direct line to Gray's newly developed telephone, but there it is nonetheless. Bell, ever the competitor, was in the airplane races as well as the telephone one and probably a bunch of others like the can-opener race and the whatever-hot-inventors-at-the-time-were-up-to race.

THE VERY CANADIAN REBELLION OF UPPER CANADA

WHAT WE **NEED** IS A REBELLION!

HEAR HEAR!

JUST A SMALL ONE. I DON'T WANT TO MAKE A FUSS

THEY'LL GET THE IDEA

HURRAH!

EDITORIAL CARTOON

HEY ST. PETER! I WAS A CELEBRITY. BUT I DIED.

A CELEBRITY!

I'M SUPPOSED TO SAY SOMETHING FUNNY

TAKE YOUR TIME

SHOW SOME RESPECT

WHERE IS THE JESTER, I COULD DO WITH SEEING SOME POINTLESS NONSENSE

HONEY, **PLEASE**! THE MAN IS AN **ARTIST**

A DURP DURP

ODYSSEUS AND HIS CREW ENCOUNTER THE FACEBOOK PERIL

SIRENS, MEN! NO ONE CAN RESIST THEIR BEAUTY

AVERT YOUR EYES!

I CAN'T HELP IT! I HAVE TO LOOK!

I WISH GIRLS WOULD STOP MAKING THAT FACE

JOCK CITY ELECTIONS

AND I PROMISE TO POUND 30% MORE NERDS IN THIS QUARTER OVER THE LAST

MEANWHILE IN NERD TOWN

I WANT DOUBLE SECURITY IN THE LOCKER DISTRICT, BOYS!

ALWAYS THE HARDEST TIME OF THE YEAR

FRENCH REVOLUTION COMICS

A DAY RUINED

INAPPROPRIATE

Ah, the French Revolution. It's one of those things where the utter madness of it all lends itself to great comedy, usually of the madcap variety. I guess your large-scale terrors are easier to handle if someone is slipping on a banana peel.

I JUST LIKE DRAWING BABIES

OPEN MIC NIGHT AT THE REVOLUTION

I'M SURE YOU UNDERSTAND

JOHN ADAMS LIGHTENS UP

John Adams was a grouchy old fellow who enjoyed being cantankerous the whole time that he was doing important things, which is a hard way to make friends. In *1776* the musical there is a whole song number where everyone is telling John Adams to sit down and shut up because they would rather be doing anything else in the world other than listen to him talk about even more things he's unhappy with. But Adams's stubborn ways have earned him a lot of fans who realize he was a cool dude in spite of it all. And really, isn't it time we just let the man relax a little?

JACKSON

CLEAN MY BOOTS

AH, YOUNG ANDREW, I'M SORRY THE WAR HAS TAKEN YOUR FAMILY FROM YOU

PERHAPS THIS WILL BE A LESSON TO YOU IN THE VALUE OF COMPASSION

OR MAYBE IT WILL TURN YOU INTO AN INSUFFERABLE ASSHOLE

EITHER IS POSSIBLE

puff puff

OLD HICKORY

THE MEN HAVE A NICKNAME FOR YOU

REALLY!

YOU KNOW, GENERAL JACKSON IS AS TOUGH AS OLD COCK.

HE REALLY IS!

TELL THEM TO THINK OF A NEW ONE

Andrew Jackson: you love him or hate him, and not much in between. He did some good things. He brought himself up from nothing and did what he thought was best. And he did a lot of bad things. Modern folks can't really look at something like the Indian Removal Act and think, "Yeah, but maybe he was an okay dude." Don't kid yourselves either—it's not like in his time no one thought to duke it out with him when he was being a jerk. The man had so many musket balls in his body you could stick magnets to him, if magnets stuck to lead.

IT WAS A GIFT

LYNCOYA

ATTEMPTED MURDER

MAN OF THE PEOPLE

EXTRA EXTRA

This isn't to say that all early political cartoons didn't belabor the point; rather, a good deal of them had several figures in view, with an entire paragraph each coming out of their mouths. Underneath the picture was, naturally, a lengthy explanation of the joke and/or main idea. A few of them managed to be pretty sick burns all the same.

GANGSTERS

SO DARLIN, DARLIN STAND

YOU GUYS WANT TO SEE A DEAD BODY?

DAVY JONES, I MEAN, IN THE DRINK

DA BOYS WANTED TO SEND YOU A MESSAGE

YOU'VE MIXED UP GENRES

WISE GUY EH

We see something in gangsters that we like. They are all dangerous and cool and there are guns and money and cars and booze and all that stuff that is great for movies and bad for anything else. A tommy gun is such an iconic thing that you'd almost think it doesn't even shoot real bullets. The car just drives by, with someone hanging out, pointing the tommy gun at you and it just goes "rat-a-tat-tat-tat!" while you stand right where you are and cheer because you are crazy.

SLEEPTIME

SURPRISE

COURTLY LOVE

Courtly Love—so pure, so true! More pining than what the modern couple would care to indulge in, but pining is better than being bored to tears at your loom, I suppose. They say it was platonic, in that I-love-you-but-will-never-touch-you way, which seems about as likely as my platonic relationship with the Loch Ness Monster (we're just friends you guys).

GIFT WARS

INTUITION

MY FAIR LADY

SWEET SIGN OF AFFECTION

BORGIAS

Lucrezia gets a bad rap for being a good-looking lady with a dubious family during a time when that set-up meant your life was going to be scandalous whether you liked it or not! They say she had a good deal of administrative sense when it came down to it, but let's face it, that's boring news compared to your father marrying you off to all his business contacts and your brother killing them.

THE MADNESS of KING LEAR

UNREASONABLE

A WATCHED POT NEVER BOILS

King Lear is based on the life of an old king named Leir who occupies a nebulous sort of space as far as being sure of how much of his story is the real deal. We can be wary I guess, but if Old King Cole might have been a real person (*really?*), then Leir deserves a fighting chance as much as the next legendary figure.

JUST LIKE THE YMCA

CAMEO

REASON IN MADNESS

GOOD IDEA

YOUNG ADA LOVELACE

Poor young Ada. The vices of poetry were all around, and within her very blood! If I were the Lady Isabella and had to deal with Lord Byron swinging dark moods around the house and swinging what was in his pants around every human or non-human item, I might have a bad opinion of The Arts as well. Isabella was a bit of a whiz with a protractor herself anyway, we are told. Later of course, Ada became famous for doing some computery things with Charles Babbage, the mechanics of their work on the Analytical Engine being something most of us still can't completely grasp, probably because our parents didn't mind if we read a poem now and then. Thus, no doubt, our mathematical ruin.

DRACULA

DON'T GO TO THE CASTLE

HAIRY PALMS ARE A GOOD SIGN AMIRITE

Here we have Bram Stoker's *Dracula*, a book written to tell ladies that if you're not a submissive waif, society goes to hell and ungodly monsters are going to turn you into child-killing horrors and someone is going to drive a bowie knife through your heart/cut off your head/etcetera. As you deserve! Thanks, Bram! I wrote it down so as to remember it. Also: foreigners. Not sure about those guys, *amirite*? Bram's got all the tips.

THE HORROR OF THE NEW WOMAN

WHAT A TRANSFORMATION

DRACULA COMES TO ENGLAND

FIFTY BOXES OF EARTH

HOT HOT METAPHORS

FOOLPROOF

CRUSOE

SHIPWRECK

TODAY, A STRANGE MAN WASHED UP ON THE BEACH

HE WAS ALIVE.

I THINK HE COMES FROM THE LAND OF NO BATHS

You smell like feet

EDUCATION

HE KEEPS TRYING TO TEACH ME HIS WORDS

AHem! Hem aDURR you Blah om...

No thanks

AT THE SAME TIME, HE HAS NO IDEA HOW GOOD MY JOKES ARE. THAT'S TOO BAD.

Heh hah hah

Robinson Crusoe has been a children's favorite for years and years. I read it as a child and distinctly recall the impression that Crusoe and Friday were pretty good friends! Crusoe and Friday, chumming it up on the island, bonfires and Good Times. Obviously though, that notion was a little lopsided. There is that scene where Crusoe puts his foot on Friday's head and says he owns him and uh, well there's also the whole book.

NICE THREADS

TODAY THE STINKY MAN
MADE SOME NEW CLOTHES
FOR HIMSELF

Hmm

I GUESS

AFFECTION

RECENTLY HE'S TAKEN
TO PATTING ME ON THE
HEAD

WHAT IS HE, MY DAD?

DOOT DOOT and
FRIDAY Bla
and ... HUR

I'M GOING TO KICK HIM
IN THE NUTS

QUIT IT

122

MANIFEST DESTINY

BUT I THOUGHT WE WERE FRIENDS

JAVERT

JAVERT CHASES A GHOST

JAVERT CELEBRATES

Forget Jean Valjean—Javert is the real money in *Les Miserables*. Javert is like a robot in a cast of humans, not computing anything except data, not executing any motion except on the program he's running. When they finally make cyborg police, every one of them will operate like Javert and then you'll be sorry you ever even looked at that loaf of bread. Just forget about it. You're better off eating something you found in the trash, really.

JAVERT HAS TROUBLE PARSING

JAVERT IS IN SLASH FICTION

JAVERT IS IN THE WRONG MUSICAL

SLOPPY LEADERSHIP

FIBER CRAZE

THE SWEATER ISSUE

WWII MOVIE

EITHER THE WALLPAPER GOES OR I DO

WWII MOVIE II

PEARSON

CALL ME MIKE

CANADA HATES ITS HEROES

Pearson had the Little Minority Government That Could, giving people free health care, pensions, and student loans for the first time, among other achievements. He gave a lot to Canada, which we—correctly or not—like to claim as proof of some national character; he symbolizes the things we like about ourselves. If only we could go back in time now and tell that to the people who made fun of his lisp.

ELECTION

WHY DON'T YOU TRY TO LOOK COOLER- LIKE DIEFENBAKER

HE'S **COOL**?

ALL THE WAY WITH LBJ

YOU COME TO **MY** COUNTRY AND TELL **MY** PEOPLE THAT **MY** WAR IS WRONG?

I OUGHTA SHOVE YOU IN A LOCKER

WE JUST THINK YOUR WAR IS PERHAPS TOO AGGRESSIVE

YOU'RE OUT OF **LINE**

GET ME THE MOST EXPERIENCED ADVISORS IN THIS PARTY!

YES SIR

I DID NOT MEAN MACKENZIE KING'S DEAD TERRIERS

SHOO

WELL YOU **ASKED**

PEARSON YOU SHUT YOUR LISPY MOUTH ABOUT THIS BLASPHEMOUS NEW FLAG ISSUE

BUT IT WILL BE UNIFYING — AND INDEPENDENT

LEAF FLAGS DON'T UNIFY CANADIANS

THEN WHAT DOES

THE BRITISH MONARCHY

I THINK THAT'S FOR UNIFYING BRITISH PEOPLE

BRAHMS'S FIRST IMPRESSION

How could Brahms have fallen asleep at a performance by Liszt? By most accounts the guy was all Jerry Lee Lewis on the piano, banging on the keys and kicking his legs and winking at the audience and making out with women all at the same time. You'd have to be already dead to fall asleep during that.

THE ADVENTURES OF SEXY BATMAN

MEET YOUR MATCH

GARTER

Batman is fun. Batman is *so much fun*, and that is why everyone makes comics about him, even though he's supposed to be scary and serious. Case closed. Everyone can make silly Batman comics now and feel good about it. Plus, did you really pick up this book for anything but Batman and butt drawings? A marriage of two fine things, like wine and more wine.

THE SLIP

BRUCE WAYNE

CARWASH

STAKE OUT

QUEEN BESS AT TILBURY

If you were at Tilbury and Queen Elizabeth, like, burst in there all up on a horse with some gnarly armor and she was yelling about how much she kicks ass and therefore you, as her subject, can do the same, maybe you too would feel like the Spanish Armada ain't no thang. In any case, it worked pretty well for her. On top of this, whenever someone tries to attack England by sea, they do it during Storm Week, which results in many wrecked ships and many more wrecked ambitions.

1980S BUSINESSWOMAN COMICS

I think these comics are mostly the product of my childhood understanding of business ladies. You see, I was born in the 1980s, when images of boxy-shouldered, helmet-haired, red-lipstick-wearing women were striding across magazines and TV shows in giant heels, and I guess they inserted themselves into the pantheon of jobs you one day figured you could have. You know, nurse, princess, teacher, businesswoman. From the images I was familiar with, I gathered that these women: (1) did business *all the time*, or (2) if they were not doing business, they were probably exercising. Pretty fierce, but also, it kind of rules.

OFFICE HOURS

DOUBLE TASK

REST

NANCYS

What mischief is Nancy Drew getting into? I've read all the books, so I can just tell you. Join me on a series of unforgettable adventures!

RASKOLNIKOV

Ah, the disenchanted young people of today, letting the things they read go to their heads. Folly of youth! It's everything your father warned you about when you said you were getting a philosophy degree. Why couldn't you just get a trade in plumbing? Everyone needs a plumber sooner or later! Now you've gone and embarrassed yourself by killing a few people for your new principles. What on earth are we going to tell the neighbours?

THROW THEM OFF THE TRAIL

HAVE YOU HEARD OF THE RECENT MURDERS?

THEY SUSPECT!

MURDERS? YOU'RE TALKING ABOUT MURDERS? I THOUGHT I HEARD SOMEONE TELL A FUNNY JOKE—WO HA HA!

I LOVE JOKES!

FAINT

BLUNT SIDE OF THE AXE BUT OH WELL

NIGHTMARES..

OH IS THIS A SEXY DREAM?

SHE TORMENTS ME

LET ME GET MY BATHING SUIT

NO

RAZUMIKHIN MY ONLY FRIEND

RASKOLNIKOV, YOU'RE SO ILL LOOKING! WHAT'S THE MATTER, LET ME HELP YOU WITH YOUR PROBLEM

NO!

BUT WE'RE FRIENDS!

HISSSS

THOUGH I COMPLETELY FORGET WHY

BUGGER OFF

ON CRIME

I FIRST SUSPECTED YOU, RASKOLNIKOV, WHEN I READ AN ARTICLE YOU WROTE

WHAT ARTICLE

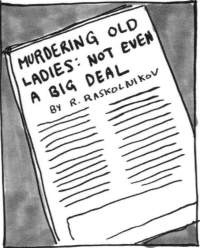

MURDERING OLD LADIES: NOT EVEN A BIG DEAL
BY R. RASKOLNIKOV

YOU ARE CLEARLY LOOKING FOR SOMETHING THAT ISN'T THERE

SONYA, GET WITH THE PROGRAM

OH SONYA, IT'S ALL BEARING DOWN ON ME, I CAN'T TAKE IT

THE GUILT OF YOUR TERRIBLE CRIMES?

TERRIBLE?? SONYA, I DIDN'T DO ANYTHING WRONG, SOMETHING **ELSE** MUST BE BOTHERING ME

YOU'RE NOT A GREAT NAPOLEON MAN AND OBVIOUSLY YOU DON'T UNDERSTAND

SAY WHAT

siiighhh

SINCE YOU BROUGHT IT UP

SIR, SIR!! ARE YOU ALRIGHT, YOU LOOK CRAZY! DO YOU NEED WATER? IS THERE...

uuughhh

ARE THERE A COUPLE OF **MURDERS** YOU NEED TO CONFESS??

NO...

WELL ACTUALLY NOW THAT YOU MENTION IT

A BRAND NEW ERA

Do you think when the Middle Ages ended, they had town meetings and everyone was instructed, "Okay, set your watches—it's the dawn of a new era"? Of course not. That's silly. No one had watches in the Middle Ages. They'd have to adjust their sundials or adjust their general sense of guessing what time of day it is.

THE FAMOUS FITZGERALDS

So, I said I would work on something with the Fitzgeralds, and here they are in all their glory, ruining each other's dreams. First Zelda got a bad rap for mucking things up for Scott, then the other way around. But the truth is, they were both a big mess. Let's call it a tie.

GREAT GATSBYS

DREAM GIRL

Everyone has to read *The Great Gatsby* in high school because it's the best example of constructing a novel with themes and symbols, like legos, only not legos but The American Dream and the eyes of Dr. T.J. Eckleburg. Fifteen-year-olds can really get behind an essay on what the green light means, which is good, because they sure as heck won't relate to any of the characters, who are all huge jerks with enough money to be wasted most of the time on top of being miserable.

LIKE TOM'S A GOOD FATHER

IN THE VALLEY OF ASHES

GREEN LIGHT

THE REAL JAY GATSBY

THAT'S PRETTY OLD

YOU CAN NEVER BE LIKE US, GATSBY. WE'RE OLD MONEY

WELL, HOW OLD?

SO OLD

OLD AS **BALLS**

LATER SHE DUMPS HIM

I'M JUST A NICE GUY, I DON'T REALLY JUDGE ANYBODY

THAT'S WHY I CAN DATE YOU, JORDAN, EVEN THOUGH YOU ARE AN ASSHOLE

AND I CAN BE FRIENDS WITH TOM EVEN THOUGH HE'S A RACIST, AND DAISY EVEN

YOU'RE TOO KIND

JUST AS GOOD THE SECOND TIME

NICK'S LUNCH DATE

HENRY'S LESSON

Wasn't it lucky for Henry that disagreeing with the Catholic Church and wanting to get rid of its power also meant pocketing a load of cash? Those monks were holy bros who prayed a lot, but they were also getting their Friar Tuck on in the Party Room of the Monasteries and Henry needed that wine money for wars and probably some wife-related funeral expenses.

HAMLET

The play *Hamlet* is a case study in the behavior of depressed young dudes during the time before you could just let off steam by listening to Morrissey records in your bedroom with the lights turned off. How many monarchs has Morrissey really saved with his music? We may never know. But what is irrefutable is that there are many less regicides these days. A connection??

CLAUDIUS AND POLONIUS ARE THERE TOO

CLAUDIUS EXPOSES HIMSELF

LAERTES RETURNS

THE PRINCE OF NORWAY ARRIVES

SACAGAWEA AND YORK TRAVEL TO THE PACIFIC

NOW WE'LL NEVER GET THERE

BACK OF THE VAN

There are people who protest the fame of Lewis and Clark because their mission didn't really do what it was supposed to, and here we are plopping them into the pages of every grade-school textbook. The real benefit of reading about Lewis and Clark is the inclusion of people like Sacagawea and York in the narrative, who were not overly remarkable in a historical sense, but were ordinary people who stood out with their courage, skills, and conviction, and did not happen to be puffed-up, high-ranking white guys, of which we already have plenty.

PAPOOSE

EARN IT

CHARBONNEAU

DESTINATION

INDUSTRIAL REVOLUTION FUN

NEW LIVING CONDITIONS

IN THE CLUB

When Oliver Twist says to the man with the food pot, "Please sir, I want some more," we know he is speaking for all the poor little orphans, and our hearts melt. Just give the little nipper some gruel! Or gravel mixed with water, whatever it was they were being fed. When your parents say, "There are starving children in Africa" to make you eat your dinner, it can only go so far. I'd throw in, "One hundred and fifty years ago you'd be a chimney sweep and dead at twelve and no one would give a shit." More broccoli please!

PLUS, IT'S CHEAP

WORK IS GOOD FOR CHILDREN, IT BUILDS THEIR CHARACTER!

GETTING MANGLED IN MACHINERY IS GOOD FOR CHILDREN, IT BUILDS CHARACTER!

LOOK AT ALL THE CHARACTER THAT CHILD HAS, HE COULD BE PRIME MINISTER!

HE'S DEAD

PREVAILING ATTITUDES

THE REASON THAT THE POOR ARE IN A BAD STATE IS NOT BECAUSE SOCIETY IS FAILING THEM

HONESTLY

IS IT **MY FAULT** THAT THEY'RE DIRTY AND LAZY?

EXACTLY EXACTLY

HONESTLY, ONCE THE POOR JUST **STOP** BEING SO **GROSS** THEY'LL BE ABSOLUTELY FINE

SO TRUE

SITCOM, VICTORIAN STYLE

RATINGS SLUMP SOLUTION

TEEN DRAMA

If you read a Victorian joke book you may be surprised by what they found funny, which is nothing, unless it was racist or sexist, in which case: hilarious. Aw, just kidding, they also thought farts were funny. If they did have a joke it took them two hours to tell it though.

A VERY SPECIAL EPISODE

WACKY NEIGHBOURS

INDEX

Kate Beaton grew up in the Maritimes, specifically Cape Breton, Nova Scotia. She earned a bachelor's degree in history and anthropology at Mount Allison University. During her last two years in school, she contributed to the student newspaper, unexpectedly morphing her lifelong obsessions with literature, history, and drawing into very funny comics. In 2007, after prodding from friends, Beaton uploaded her first comics to her website, receiving acclaim that set her on the path to becoming one of the most successful and talked about new cartoonists of the past decade. She eventually self-published the now-sold-out book *Never Learn Anything From History*. Her comics have appeared in the *New Yorker, Harpers*, the *National Post*, and *The Best American Comics* anthology. She won the Doug Wright Award for Best Emerging Talent and has been nominated for the Harvey and Shuster awards. Her website is www.harkavagrant.com.